turning to drones

Mark Young

Concrete Mist Press, 2020

turning to drones by Mark Young

ISBN #: 978-1-7344409-2-8

front cover image
geographies: Kyburra
by Mark Young

back cover photo
by Lauren Young

cover design
by harry k stammer

cont'd

Some of these poems have previously appeared in

*A New Ulster, Adelaide Literary Magazine, Angry Old Man Magazine, Anti-Heroin Chic,
BlazeVOX, coelacanth, ENTROPY, Eunoia Review, Futures Trading, Hamilton Stone Review,
in-Appropriated Press, Indefinite Space, Journal of Poetics Research, London Grip, New Mystics,
Noon: journal of the short poem, otata, Oz Burp 5, Right Hand Pointing, Silver Pinion,
Stride magazine, SurVision, Synchronized Chaos, The Curly Mind, The Lake,
The Writing Disorder, Unlikely Stories Mark V, Utsanga.it, X-Peri, & Yellow Mama.*

My thanks to the various editors.

An introduction to a book of dreams

I am writing the

introduction to a

book of dreams. This

is the first dream.

The extinct river

He collected water
from different rivers,
from the same river
at different times. Kept
in a controlled environment
to prevent evaporation. In
old jam jars. Numbered.
Carefully registered.
Date, place, sometimes

season. Whether up-
or downstream from some
notable landmark. The
Fitzroy, 12/17/96, 2 km
above the Barrage, on
the third day of rain. Or:
Nine Mile Creek, seven
years of silence & then
the first flow. 1/13/79.

Most now clear water for
the sediment settles over
time. Different levels of
it, sometimes a sequence,
often sad. Thirty-three years
of the Murray, the jars
side by side, the first with
a thin layer of silt, the last
a jar of desiccated dust.

Un aperçu does not a swallow make

The odalisque that peers
through the attic window
is jealous of me, even
though he has *foie gras*! I
make do with donkey
dung, or the tongues of
vipers, or an admonished
army advocate-general

trying to perceive the truth
of natural selection in every
review of the ranks. But each
is a singular meal when
served with gentle music
towed from across the bay.

Compline

R.E.M. in the background, in front
of which trains, flooded rivers,
the taste of a night filled to the brim
with misplaced articles of faith.

charges of *Frankenfood* are heard in the land

Advocates of decentralization
agree that this snippet from a
US rifle website is much more
than a slow dance of Polish origin,
is part of a genetically modified
affliction that dismembers relation-
ships when rendered in 3/4 time.

Is fashion a form of expression?

This year, during Elvis Week,
officials working as part of a
team hope culling the habitat-
altering cormorants will save

an eco-system & finally allow
nightclubs to have everything
needed to ensure refreshment &
entertainment are close at hand.

Marduk had his first real swim today

Levi-Strauss' answer was to
crowdsource a venture-capital

enterprise affiliated with the
Royal Canadian Mounted Police

which then approved about $400
billion in supplemental spending

for the thin horizontal pinkish-
purplish lines on my monitor.

Each bowl

The container is double-layered.
How much time should be allowed
for it to fester can often be deduced
from the interplay between the two
materials. Soon we will be offering
small pieces of really old ships. Let's
see if that does the trick. We have relo-
cated to a place just outside the village,

hoping we can find a cheap place to
rent, away from the nightclubs but
still have close by everything needed
to guarantee a continuous source of
entertainment. The evenings are
often given over to passion & prayer.

Small benchtops & a stenchcore band

There are bikers who are joining in
on Saturday. The brix levels are
already good. Small cinnamon sticks
with slices of apple had preciously
caused quite a few problems with
the retrieval of geo-spatial data; but the
growing tendency of parents to give
projects based around lexical statistics

means dictionaries will pop up before
you're even halfway into the entry
vestibule. Such virtuosity is the culmi-
nation of long years of hard work. We
have ambushed the mainstream. Now
cellos thrive as the vibration baseline.

Within your organization

A new partnership brings sports
&, at some random point, a girl's
coronation doll. Music can inspire,
but avoid tuna if you react badly
to it. Since the numbers are wrong,
why am I bothering to reproduce
them. The beginning was saccharine:
the markets had all closed: future-

proof secondary packaging carried
warnings to be wary of false prom-
ises. Spring's manifestations become
the basis for the creation of a frame-
work for turning New York City into an artifact from fifteenth century.

pre-Colombian parentheses

It is hypothesized that the widespread use of chemical batteries
will result in efficiency increases
for any human who rides a bicycle.
Something about a conflation of
music & power, both of which can
be seen as a series of 'lines' on
photographic film. The literature

on the subject is immense, usually
in high quality peer-reviewed full-
text publications, & embellished
with consumer reviews & price com-
parisons. Comes in genuine leather, &
features elastic to restrain your Kindle.

The / main reason / for their misfortune

No such thing as information
hardware when you go skinny-
dipping. All soft, no mix &
match, show some flesh or show
nothing at all. It's a crucial mode
of conception, where symbols are
kept in a cupboard for disciplinary
reasons. The lotus flower becomes

a horse with little energy. Whose
saddle cuts in, a social vulnerability, dressed & wearing a new
landscape that has the texture of
natural hair in order to pretend
it isn't just another creation myth.

Leaving behind your familiar house

Winter on the mainland can
be an enormously stressful
time. Antelopes stand on their
hind legs to reach the acacia
leaves, hoping to break the Yin
or Yang down into its essential
five elements. Freud hid his work
from Jung at first, considered it

a difficult & painful topic, something he wasn't comfortable
talking about to his mother. Instead offered up a compilation
of therapy tips & techniques
gleaned from 17 years training.

Are you stressed and lethargic? Caught
inside a perfectly rectangular block?
Under no obligation to obey the laws
of ethics or morality? Born with no
innate or built-in mental content?
Seem to have a limited lifetime? Refer
to landscaping in ways that do not
require supplemental irrigation? Fill

the Incense Cup with rice chaff ash
& do not compact? Talk of crystal
chandeliers in a fundamentally different way? Use an opposition such
as "nature/culture" as a tool while not
accepting it as philosophical truth?

If any response is positive, use the Phase One plan

image track

The brain grows tired from
being out in the sun. He sits
listening to an extremely cool
version of a heat exchanger,
wonders about the trade-in
value of a montage of cash-
mere twin-sets with pearls,
decides that additional in-

vestigation must be made into nanoparticle ontology. That's
where he stopped, suddenly
aware of the similarity between
mobility issues & the susurrus
of child protection safety seats.

after touring your war museum

The Romans & the Arabs —
oddly & exotically — built
seaside towns filled with
guttered fields for grow-
ing rice in. But ever since
gift shops destroyed those
first attempts & allowed the
bubonic plague entry into

Europe, the principle of
asymmetry no longer holds.
Flags may be flown at night
only when fish or ducks or
any other actor in the economy
is suffering from a food allergy.

barbican

I don't know why : to
promote myself

I don't know when : my
anxiety level has been pushed to an historical high

Please use this display : as
a guideline with unique items : or as
a standardized way to manipulate the browser

: don't interfere with anything :

Your comment has been saved : but
will not appear until approved by :

the author : or

by Police in the US state of Missouri

wagasa

Idiosyncrasies float by below
me. The bridge ignores them,
instead turns & offers me

an *ukiyo-e* woodblock print
of the Sanjo Bridge that spans
the Kamo River. I hold it up

to the light. "Quite the self-
portrait," I say, "even though
it is of another time & place."

the shallow ocean floor

Make your own website, quickly.
Reconcile such a dramatic economic
year. Forget that planned journey
to Damascus on Monday; instead
visit the Angel City Bookstore in
Santa Monica. Has anyone tried
& was successful at Globalization?

Great landscapes of history

4/192 Charters Towers Rd

next door to The Cheesecake
Shop

same complex as
Radio Rentals
a pizza shop

Athenian Plaza
~~next door~~

Top Brand Cycles

The pedestrian bridge

The female goes nude
to bed, wears wire
mesh in the hope she'll

morph into a docuseries
in which four men con-
template colonialism &

wonder if they'd feel the
same about it if it came in
a variety of pastel shades.

The final word

He avoided flying. The mall
was air-conditioned. How could

she have been so stupid. The clouds
were gathering, storm colors, in nat-

ural skin tones, based on status &
dreams. The heat made the pave-

ment soft, forensic reports spewed
from the coffee machine. The person

she usually shared the room with was
overseas. She enjoyed the privacy.

monkey canapes

In order to stop kids
obsessing over the future,
Government funding is

now available to separate
them into groups &
place them on a range of

intimate couches in front
of refrigerators which all
have smart screens & apps.

Re-reading Ashbery

The back &
forth of
poetry.

I forgot to post
the sky a letter.

The moon did not
come. All day

the sun. Darkness.

justifiable taco

Rewriting the blueprint doesn't
always work. Big Data can be
a little messy; but a cocktail will
balance out the calories. There's

no reason for a grown-ass man
to use the acronym IMHO unless
he's attracted by the arguments
of outsider, populist politicians.

Deconstructing Dickens

It was the best of
times—all the big-
name philosophers
were in the room.

It was the worst
of times—he didn't
understand a word
they were saying.

A Small Compendium

High summer
is such an
elegant phrase

but he kept
a small
compendium
of winter

on hand
for days

like this.

La physique quantique

Have you stopped asking questions about yourself?

Have you stopped questioning the answers?

When you see yourself reflected in a mirror
do you move out of the line of sight? Or do you

accept the presence of the other & then move on?

Nathalie Montressor (1824-1851): from *Les Allusions d'optique*
translated by Umberto Allegrezza

[archival footage]: The Bush / Kerry debate

Like a
comedy
of manners

or a
masque
where one

protagonist
wears the face
of a weasel

& the other
the face of
a horse.

Trepanned

After the inserts
were all in place
she fell asleep in

a dodecahedral
envelope. Summer
bounded by like an

holographic ante-
lope. Grass fell. It
burned her eyes.

Survivisection

A coal stove burns
in the corner. I don't
want a coal stove. In
a survival situation,
versatility is essential.

Knife, ax & machete –
these items are extremely
necessary. Other minimal
lists have taken the count-
ing challenge to the limit.

I now own 15 things. *Je
veux un hamburger.* "Yes.
Much as I expected." The
other eats, hates himself
for eating, & then purges

it out. Houses are the best
places to hide out in. I exit
out of the tail with CTRL+C
& continue. Assume that
everything is case specific.

My biggest fear is that I'll
fall back down the hole.
Ramen noodles aren't the
most nutritional food but
they are cheap. & easy to

prepare. I no longer have
a coal stove or pots & pans
or water, but I watched
a video & now know how
to cook ramen in a cactus.

The young Han Solo

describes the past decade
as a really tumultuous

time for the beef industry

but he is excited about
what the future holds.

A / first pressing / or a reissue?

The men who now assume to rule the
country have themselves become

the victims of corruption. They are
beginning to regret the departure

of the Egyptians. A singular lack
of *fingerspitzengefühl* isn't the only

way to find oneself defending the
expectation of unlimited violence.

Indolent concrete

is a regular process, but has much
more waffle plus a high-pitched
whine. Natural curiosity spawns
certain small renal masses that seem
in need of a novel defense. What can
we do? The foundational grounds

of European civilization no longer
satisfy, no longer serve as heuristic
tools. Nor can the neighbors, just
moved in, who are so bland & un-
interesting that any curiosity about
them would have to be unnatural.

The chains coil up into helical structures

The logo tells a story. It's
a two-faced model, much
like Janus, which the de-
signers promise will create
a deep connection with the
masses. The α helix, beloved
by scientists, faces inward;
it was the first metal used by

man; more than seven-in-ten
think it is of greater import-
ance than buying the latest
iPhone or a new BMW. I like
traditional business models.
They emit toxic by-products.

Line Thirteen

I don't want to
come back to a room
that's empty of
everything except
enmity. I don't want
to come back to a
room that's full of
corners that can't
contain me. The two
are not mutually
exclusive. Some-
thing to do with
sympathetic magic.

carrying the banner

At various intervals, in
this host of decibels
& sfxed arena, an
ordinary-looking man
comes up on stage to
shake a tambourine, in
tune, & on time.

Land / Rover is / what we do

Having a thread go
& reload the data
caused a race condition.

Stale bread can be
turned into croutons.

I got a small vanilla latte.

The transition of Cold-Dryness

I really love getting my
eyebrows done by my
psychiatrist. I have not

eaten all day; have gently
filled my colon with warm
filtered water; have spent

the afternoon filling in
crossword puzzles. Years
pass quickly & my eye-

brows keep growing. Time
to visit my shrink & fill
the room with foul odors.

prices & dates should be used as a guide only

Any self-assembly of living
matter that can eliminate
both noise from the

optical field & erosion
caused by repeated firing
in the vent of a gun

redefines a market
segment that would other-
wise have little value.

TRANSCENDENCE

Total energy narrowly circum-
scribes. Creates frontiers &
borders. Characterized by the
need to have an entire body
of knowledge devoted to it.

Embodied energy goes any-
where, with anything. Never
goes out of style except within
the environs of the *Leichen-
haus*, the Hospital for the Dead.

since violence is learned

The library platform is indepen-
dent in all sections, apart from the
young adult ministry niche. That's
involved in environmental manage-
ment matters — such as: can a fully
veiled woman purchase a vehicle? —
in addition to training multilingual
staff to assist you with debugging

problems, & providing tour & ticket
assistance. Soldiers encourage the
youth to attend. The more aged &
less mobile are taken away to be dis-
posed of thoughtfully. Tolerance is no
longer available, is replaced by trauma.

teflon eyes

Preschoolers get apple juice
at snack time. I just wanted
to exchange my eyes for the
teflon pair he kept in the desk
drawer. Plenty of these tools
have become available even
on the clear web; but he was
selfish with his, refused to give

them to me. We both got angry,
came to blows, took out our
knives. The potential fallout
could extend far beyond West
Virginia. Getting him on camera
would have been a scene saver.

Potato chips

> Nothing proceeds as
> intended. Idolatry
>
> prevails, some sort of
> distraught calculus
>
> in which the trumpets
> go on strike the mo-
>
> ment that the camels
> enter the courtyard.

complicated transactions involving middlemen

How many schools have
their own Crash Test
facility with a deep voice,
& big eyes & mouth? The
potential is horrendous, but
wearing a sexy Red Riding
Hood costume on the school
fun run has nothing to do with
the education of the students.

A sequence for Gary Snyder

The female is not al-
ways fertile — these
offerings are testament
to that, mounds of
colored rice left in the
laps of carved gods.

*

At night the temple
gates close. By morn-
ing the rice is gone.

*

The rich use saffron &
paper plates. All the
poor can afford is wild
turmeric & banyan leaves.

*

The better the gift the
more chance of conception
is what the priests say.
What the priests say
is not heard by the gods.

*

They have no interest in
rice, leave that for the
priests' dinner. Their

concern is with the yellow
fingerprint stains left by
the women on the offering

platters. Tracing the whorls
to see what is written there
of the supplicant's future.

*

"It is a difficult dance to do."

Prelude to a *ficcione*

The name of Francis Roche does not appear in the list of
musicians who took part in the Miles Davis / Gil Evans album
"Sketches of Spain." He was meant to have been there, was meant
to have played the bass clarinet lines that lie like an echo under
the melancholy of Miles as he begins the adagio of Joaquín
Rodrigo's *Concierto de Aranjuez*. Instead, someone else is there. I
cannot bring myself to find out who.

A robber in the habit of spilling secrets

Trending newborns come
in an assortment of chic
patterns—the New Year sure

did bring a hefty dose of celeb-
rity baby-bumpin' news. But
this is Apple, after all, & what

the inventors did not factor in
was that a trained fighter would
be awaiting them when they

attempted to stick-up the latest
sign of opposition to the US
military presence on Okinawa.

Leaving the Motorway

She asks one last question.
They walk up the stairs.

He finally stops near a
construction shed. Call me

if you need help. She had
not been ill, that much was

clear. Nor had she acted poli-
tically although a complaint

against her had once been
made. It was in the archives.

indentured caravans

We rarely think about
eating disorders when we

talk about nocturnal

dumpster diving in the
gay male community.

Sorry, but I couldn't find a bottle

Try not to read too much into it. Certainly elephants are rare in these parts, & elephants giving birth even more so. But remember that here you're on the main road from nowhere to nowhere; & at the somewheres in between anything is a possibility.

After all there are still supposed sightings of the Tasmanian tiger & the local version of the yeti / sasquatch. Yowies they call them here. Just say to the Tourist Bureau on your way out of town that you saw a pachyderm. Anywhere else they might be astute enough to ask if it was Indian or African & get suspicious when you can't tell them where the tusks were relative to the ears.

Here they'll just record it as an unconfirmed sighting & include it in their next brochure as another reason to visit North Queensland. &, hopefully, someday someone out there in the Great Beyond will see the tourist brochure, recognize the hand behind the inherent absurdity of the claim, & say "So that's where Mark Young is living now."

Half a *ficcione* is better than no *ficcione* at all

Having bent time,
gone into the future
& noted how they
fell, Albert Einstein

won lots of money
playing the cards as
he foresaw them. Ob-
servers reported he

was hoppier than a
pig in mud. "It's all
relative," he said. "At
least, that's the theory."

marked with an icon

Working in partnership with the
inhabitants of Key Largo, we become
more conscious of both child pass-
enger safety & the attraction of a
natty new black T-shirt displaying
the message "open from 10:00 a.m.
to 5:30 p.m., but investment in new
facilities is currently unavailable."

It's a script so long it runs over onto
the wearer's back, breaking — dependent
on the size — after either the given
times or before the last two words.
Operators of heavy machinery are
often inclined to wear it inside out.

Paging Darwin

An internal investigation into
the goanna's supply chain

reveals that the widely-held
belief that its hierarchy of IT-

related capabilities functions
using three dimensions of inte-

gration is not only wrong but it is,
overall, a far less efficient reptile

than the similarly-named but un-
related inhabitants of Central &

South America plus some isolated
islands off the coast of Ecuador.

A note for Alex Gildzen

<pre>
        Giving my
        age away
        is this ay-
        em's un-
        bidden
        offering
        from the un-
        conscious
        jukebox in my
        mind—The
        Andrews Sisters
        singing *Bei Mir
        Bist Du Schoen.*
</pre>

The bebop bird

This morning, amongst the raucous caws of the crows, the harsh shrieking of the white cockatoos, & the shrill trills of the magpie larks, I heard a bebop bird. *Drlllll do be dlop / a dulya dop, drlllll do be dlop / a dulya dop*.....that's how it went, sort of like the tunes Benny Golson used to do with Art Blakey &, later, The Jazztet — not those lyrical pieces such as *Whisper Not* or *I Remember Clifford* but the laidback ones like *Killer Joe* that include a point when the ensemble stops, the soloist comes in, & the drummer goes back to heightening that fourth beat of the bar. 1 2 3 clock, 1 2 3 clock. All that's missing here.

questions, questions

Sting on the
way in is
fine, but how

do I feel about
Tina Turner grunt
& groaningly

pacing my
exit from the
shopping mall?

The

    allocation of
        energy

is easy
        when there is

    no energy
left to
        allocate.

fortuitous onslaught

Aleister Crowley &
his deviant ways ex-

emplified the greatness
of the Roman Empire.

I. II. XIII

Intrigue, or the

      application of
sympathetic magic
to unsympathetic

      sights & sites.

So little

happened
there, he
    gave the
    frogs

    names
    & lived
vicariously
through them.

at least six toxic gases

The Galaxy came to Toyota
Stadium on Saturday afternoon. This was their chance,
as we embarked on a new
century, to give a gift of great
value to future generations.
Turned out our browser
didn't recognize any of the
video formats currently available & the opportunity was lost.
Spectators under the control
of the Post & Telegraph depart-
ment were forced to pay a fee.

Seismic Performance

Use case studies to isolate
a single locale to exhibit
multiple motions, then segue

into an ancient Chinese secret
over 5000 years old, that YSL
lovers wake up & go to bed

wearing his clothes. That
since his passing many of
them now feel like orphans.

Stuck inside of Mobile

I want too much, &
often take the same.

Economists tell me
this is wrong, a part

of it anyway, for
wants are unlimited

but resources scarce.
& so my prolifigacy

will cause prices to rise,
babies to starve, atolls

in the South Pacific to
submerge as temper-

atures increase in anger
at my actions. I turn away,

want not to know what
my wants might lead to.

Crystal clear transparency

Neither the cache middleware nor
the transmission of sound signals
through space is perceived as anti-
assimilationist. Yet, at the blessing
of their colors in St. Isaac's Cathedral
on June 21st, just before they left for
the front, both operators claimed
absolute moral privilege to present

obviously doctored case studies in
order to exclude anyone wishing
to audition for the Randy Squirrel
Theater Group from the electoral
rolls. Nothing stood up to scrutiny.
Women stand outside in protest.

a tropical sunset

I am one of those conserv-
atives who has decided
that practicing self-love in

secret is a misreading of
Hegel. I know the link
between systemic failure

& the vasodilatory effects
of sexual misconduct is not
defined at this time; but still

think it provides a genuine
though theoretical alternative
to mainstream economics.

The coexistence of mutiple strains

Forget about the conservation of the hair,
especially when compared to a terres-
trial bacteria, the only survivor of a
group that was globally widespread
at the time of the dinosaurs. Their
process of formation demonstrates
the vulnerability of communities &
populations to natural hazards. Might

also exhibit the characteristics of poetry,
especially when recorded in an aband-
oned house in the hills of Kentucky
with strands of iodine added to eke
out the conceptual model. The theme is
mirrors. With mirrors often come masks.

Dear Evolution.

The energies displayed by you
allow me to finance foreign
exchange interventions & to
depict in profile those objects

that have some relationship
with either coffee beans or
turf sold for home lawns, be

it mathematical or simply the
outcome of a new collective
bargaining agreement con-
nected by cable to a serial port.

He had killed his brother

An elephant goes on a rampage:
its center was a step cut citrine;
looked strangely like a toy.

As far as motor skills are concerned,
cognitive & interpersonal skills are
needed to manage matching parasols.

My home was destroyed by an earth-
quake. This nonlinear pattern also offers
a key iconographical spotlight shining

right on you. The differences appear to
have become lost. Some *mah song* men-
acingly slice their tongues with axes. Years

later I have recreated myself. The technical
obstacles to reconstruction are immense.

A sharp examination

Recognizing a single locus
he said, again & again,
with deftness & wonder,

"I saw her a year ago.

"Small details like artistic
event space let her avoid
culture & defy logic & fear."

This kind of operation, we were
told, causes very intense pain.

It has seen too many
burned down homes.

neither wave nor particle

Is said, *sans* apps, a PC is
a typewriter, a smartphone
a slab of glass — but those are

false dichotomies for other
options are available. Like.
Get your meme on, with a block

of text. Meme may be a dirty
word in every language but is
a crucial element for success.

dense cover

Because of
contiguity

: it has advantages :
: is entitled (to)

: unless reshaped
into some greater

: thing, special :
: a \ legend / :

rendered the plan
redundant.

Without a Trace

He leaned in front of her
screen. Then he made himself

more comfortable. The dead man
was hanging close to the trunk.

She was thirsty, but that was
not unusual; & if she needed

company then a row of half-dead
plants still lined the pathway.

home aclone

I have dismantled the cloning machine. So much
promised, so little gained. So many copies of me
out there I have lost count & lost control.
                                        I think
it was the me emerging as a sumo wrestler
who broke the meter some years ago — although
it could have been that other time when I came
out as an androgyne & it couldn't decide if none
or one or two copies had been delivered.
                                        Much
of the proliferation derives from the night
the junkie me nodded off & left the machine
to spit out so many copies it eventually depleted
the toner & invisible mes continued to disappear
through until morning.
                        Two things in retrospect.
I should never have built in the ability to produce
alternative identities nor should I have let those
altered copies make copies of themselves. It
accelerated the chromosome decay, grew the
damage exponentially. George H.W. Bush's
Parkinson's is particularly pronounced but he
is old. Robin Williams' came much sooner. Britney
Spears' is still to show.
                        I have learnt my lesson far
too late; now I am in clear & present danger (note
to myselves: good title for a novel). Each day
the threats increase. So obvious that the newer
ones don't like me; & if you knew me like / they
know me you'd know that that's not like me at all.

Constant Craving

The day is spinning wildly
on its turntable, & even out
of it the vibrations can still
be clearly felt. I'm trapped in
what might as well be Mach-
iavellian Merchandise, a tent
in sideshow alley, where there's
nothing you want or need
or can afford but still feel
compelled to spend up big before
you go. Either by the purchase of
a cutprice epiphany that is not
yet spoken for—which in itself
is indicative of its value—or doing
a dodgy deal in wagyu beef
futures. Neither of which...

But I am brought down to
earth & saved from calamity
by a track squeezing through
from the dodgems next door,
k.d. lang singing *so in love,* the
Cole Porter song, that acts as
axis to steady everything around.

Still can't figure out what to buy for that special someone?

Fashion designers be-
come inspired in those
first rigorous
conditioning workouts

when they're called
upon to coil a
rope on the ground &
within its confines re-

place the DNA structure
of several named Hindu
deities with a mixture of
spinach, raisins, & lean beef.

a mantra for nights when there's a full moon

wolfgang   masochist   footbridge
conundrum burial bode apprise visual
agway vitriol vanderpoel apart bawdy
husbandry communion amoral kapok
neutron kennecott ale wing emphysema
heinrich plod schoolbook stoic chaise
gangplank   anteroom   quadrangular
descendant   commend   amphibious
covary era

muscovite   sabotage   disposable
accentual backlog traceable contiguity
boyfriend airspace net bohr excavate
bacilli   donner   dimension   invoice
premiere   biochemic   cheeky   annal
dominate bullyboy della lunch idyllic
baneful ariadne annette babble fluke
debugged assign engineer fermentation
criminal copy pygmy

cotillion deflect hilly geology leap
plenum   applique   derision   curtsey
assyria   deign   quadrangle   arrack
millionth agglutinate ike dickens falter
decent fedders jeannie clarke australia
employee   changeable   graduate
pathology   architect   tuberculin
bennington   recuperate   humphrey
monocotyledon civet

persian belfast basal algorithm lipid
republic briefcase complicate behold
cloudy dowling thoroughgoing meant
spheric bureaucrat diploidy ashland
osgood   dean   reef   contradistinct
withheld   beset   profligacy   beloit
algorithmic stillwater predatory amount
deprivation plenty gigavolt stipple
townsmen rapture dearborn caribbean
retard

The Owls

There's always an audience
out there. It's just that sometimes you've got to go out
on a limb to pull them in.

Don't be subtle about it. Start
by covering the exterior walls
of your house with sheets of
corrugated iron painted in

primary colors. Wait until round
about midnight, then walk out
into the garden & begin reciting
your poems. This will infuriate

the owls. Poetry confuses them.
They're sure to retaliate, lay shit
on your renovations, stare at you
with those big wide eyes they

have & say: *You should have used
wood or adobe.* Or: *A delicate shade
of lime would have been much more
relaxing.* But keep at the poems

until the owls have finished
hooting at you, then point out
how the colors now make it easier
for them to separate the mice

from the surrounding shrubbery.
They will pause, then nod. It'll
be faint praise, but at least you
won't be damned by it, & with

a reliable food supply available
the owls will stick around. People
will come to see them. Some may
even stay & listen to your poetry.

A / little something / for Ray Craig

The temperament
of birds. Cardboard
containers of take-
out noodles. Light,
elongated? No, not
that, the things it
touches. Ensuing.

The azaleas

Even though I
could not sleep
& even though
the solar lights
stayed on all
night & even
though we plant-
ed them together,
I always found

an excuse why
not to visit when
he rang up in
the early hours
of the morning
& invited me
around to see
how the azaleas
were coming on.

turning to drones

The Dutch pack up. The exodus
gathers pace. Now there are
empty houses & jobless maids.

The funerals begin. Allow ample
time for parking & to rubberneck
the tornado damage. Studying

bees could help. They understand
zero & can do basic math. They
deserve respect, say the scientists.

Made in the USA
Monee, IL
24 February 2020